Radical Family Workbook and Activity Journal for Parents, Kids and Teens

Radical Family Workbook and Activity Journal for Parents, Kids and Teens

Written by teens, this is a totally new approach to the traditional family meeting with activities to bond, connect and inspire families of all kinds.

Vanessa Van Petten

iUniverse, Inc.
New York   Bloomington

Radical Family Workbook and Activity Journal for Parents, Kids and Teens
Written by teens, this is a totally new approach to the traditional family meeting
with activities to bond, connect and inspire families of all kinds.

iUniverse books may be ordered through booksellers or by contacting:

iUniverse
1663 Liberty Drive
Bloomington, IN 47403
www.iuniverse.com
1-800-Authors (1-800-288-4677)

Because of the dynamic nature of the Internet, any Web addresses or links contained in this book may have changed since publication and may no longer be valid.

ISBN: 978-1-4401-9177-0 (sc)
ISBN: 978-1-4401-9178-7 (ebk)

Printed in the United States of America

iUniverse rev. date: 12/10/2009

INTRODUCTION:

Welcome!

I am so excited that you are taking this leap. The Radical Family Workbook will be challenging, but incredibly rewarding, fun and inspiring. Myself, Vanessa Van Petten and 20 of my teen interns created it.

In this series, we put together 30 sessions worth of challenges and activities to help your family re-start, re-energize and re-connect.

In each session, families will get a set of challenges, materials and action steps to do for about 30 minutes. Families can work through the Radical Family Workbook at their own pace! You could do a session every day or one every three months!

This is for families with children of all ages. Younger children can even participate in many of the activities and family bonding times.

STRUCTURE:

The book is broken into 30 sessions. You can complete these at your own pace. It is best if you can do these on a consistent schedule, whether that is once a week, once a month or every other month. Continuity helps you not forget what you have been working on.

We also recommend skimming ahead and previewing some of the topics just to get an idea of the cool stuff you have ahead.

When you are ready to do a session:

1) Sit down with your entire family in a quiet and comfortable place.

2) Fill in the date before each session. You want to remember when you completed each task so when you read this journal years down the line you can remember when you were completing it!

3) Read the short introductory paragraph about the goal of the session and what you should keep in mind.

4) Complete the tasks and activities listed for you.

5) Journal: When you see the "Journal:" mark, you want to read the questions and either write in your answers in your personal journal or just discuss your answers.

6) Read and plan how you will complete your homework assignments which are listed at the end of each session.

Remember this is all at your own pace. If there is a question or topic you are uncomfortable with, feel free to change it, modify it or skip it. The goal of this workbook is to get your family to bond, grow and reconnect.

*We do leave some space within the book to answer the journals and questions, but you might want to consider getting an extra blank pad of paper for each family member to keep with the Radical Family Workbook and answer the journal questions there so you have plenty of space!

Session 1: Get on Board

Date:

This is probably the first time many of your family members will have heard about this project. This workbook is a series of activities and exercises that should be fun, inspiring and interesting for your family to do together.

Task 1: Who decided to get this workbook? Please tell the group what motivated you to get it and why you wanted to do it.

Task 2: Discuss the project goals together. Then add a few of your own.

Project Goals:

1. Learning to be honest with each other

2. Communicating the hard stuff

3. Changing bad patterns

4. Having more fun as a family

5. Asking for what you need

6. Getting to know each other

7. Getting to know yourself

8.

9.

10.

Task 3: Read through the contract together in the Tools Section. Sign the contract and add your own points.

JOURNAL:

Each family member should answer in their personal journals or discuss their answers.

What are you dreading most about doing this workbook?

What are you most excited about?

ASSIGNMENTS:

__Figure out where you want to have your Family meetings on a regular basis

__Figure out how regularly you want to meet and do an activity. Put this in your family and personal planners and calendars.

SESSION 2: FAMILY MEETINGS

Date:

Essentially, each family session is a family meeting. We hope that you will carry on the family meetings even after you are done with all of the activities in this workbook. Our teens suggested that each family meeting should have a basic structure. In this session we will set up how you want your family meetings to run and then begin to carry out those tasks before you do the activities in future sessions.

Family meetings are crucial because:
- They keep communication open

- You can stay updated on every family member's needs

- It is a great moment to look back at what has happened in the past month for your family

- They help you make the next month better!

Task 1: Go through what we recommend for every family meeting and our sample agenda.

What Every Family Meeting Should Have:

1) Announcements and Check-in

2) Review of Goals

3) Complaints and grievances?

4) Kudos and Rewards

(5) Session Video, Assignments)

6) Goals for next month

1) Announcements and Check-in: The meeting should start off with everyone going around and saying if they have any announcements. This is also a time for them to reflect about their month.

One of the major parts of family-check-ins is teaching kids to be able to reflect on what is going on for them. This helps them check-in with themselves, be grateful and appreciate the moment.

If you have a teen or child who insists that "there are no announcements or updates and the month was 'fine'" then I would build in discussion points. Like having everyone rate their month from 1-5 and telling the high point, the low point and a random fact...this gives them something to focus on.

2) Goals: This is a really important part of family meetings. Teaching kids how to make goals is an important skill. I think the family as a whole can also have goals. We have a few full sessions on goal making coming up. When going around each person should talk about their goal and their progress on it. Someone can take notes in your goal log (explanation to come) to keep track of progress.

3) Complaints and Grievances: This is an essential part of the meeting. This can be difficult to hear, but it is important to teach your kids how to exercise their anger or frustration in a constructive and helpful way. Go around in a circle and have people bring up issues, or events that have upset or bothered them in the last month. Then it is important for all family members to talk them through and see how it would be better for next month. In my family, it went something like this:

> *Brother: "I am upset because I feel like I am two years older than Vanessa, but she still gets to go to bed at the same time as me. I did not have that when I was her age."*

> *Mom: "Ok, what time did you go to bed when you were her age? And what time would you like to go to bed? Vanessa would you be upset about going to be 30 minutes earlier?"*

> *Vanessa: "Yes! I do not want to go to bed at 10:30, I need my 11pm bedtime for homework."*

> *Mom: "I do not think it is fair to lessen Vanessa's bedtime after she has already had 11pm and I think 11:30pm is too late for you."*

Dad: "How about you can stay up to 11pm only if you are reading or doing homework. Robert can stay up until 11pm, but he can watch TV before bed because he is older."

This compromise really helped everyone feel heard and avoided fights at 10:30pm at night when my brother thought it was unfair that I was staying up. Everyone should go around and list any complaints or grievances.

4) Kudos and Rewards: This is when everyone goes around and has to give someone kudos for something, like picking up laundry, making curfew on time or maintaining their goal. Rewards are usually dolled out by parents and this depends on the family. Sometimes this was going out for donuts after the meeting, sometimes this is when my parents would announce a family vacation or hand out allowance.

5) Stay consistent: If you are going to do this, do it well! Do it every month no matter what (we have done them in airports) and make sure to stick to the agenda. Make sure everyone participates and set a good example with your goals. This is the same principal as being consistent with the family activity book.

6) Make your tweaks: If you are going to make new rules and you have had trouble keeping them in the past, consider:

-Parent kid contracts

-A family bulletin board.

-Email alerts and reminders and program them in together.

-Talking stick. If you have a loud family, have a talking stick so no one can talk over each other.

-Start your meeting with a silly question, conversation starter or icebreaker.

Again, every person is different, make family meetings personalized to your family. This is a great way to maintain close bonds and communication with family members. The typical family meeting agenda should accompany the activities for that session that we assign for you.

Do you want to do anything special in your meetings that we have not listed here?

Task 2: Fill in the "Our Family Meeting Agenda" in the Tools Section. Write what you want to do and a short description of each activity so you can use it in future meetings in case you forget.

Task 3: Actually carry out the items on your family meeting agenda for the first time. Skip the goals section until we get to the goals session!

We always leave you space to take notes on your family meetings. This helps later to follow up with family members and also is fun when looking back at the journal for what was going on for each family member at this point in their lives.

Family Meeting Notes:

Journal:

Do you think your family will be able to do all of the sessions without quitting, why or why not?

What can you do to insure you will stick to your family meeting agenda?

Assignments:

__Get a large wall/fridge calendar for next time.

__Get some supplies for your next family meeting:

*white paper

*pencil case with pens, pencils, highlighters

*post-its

*paper-clips

Session 3: Roles

Date:

We think that having each family member participate in different parts of the family meeting and growth is essential…and fun! In this session we are going to assign roles to different family members, even young ones. You should rotate these roles every 3 sessions to give everyone a chance to try all of the roles. Once everyone has had one turn in a role, you can keep rotating or swap to stay in your favorites.

Task 1: Go through the roles and make sure everyone understands them.

Roles:

1) <u>Project Leader</u>: Project leader has many advantages, they get to settle compromises and can be in charge of arranging when to have family meetings. They also get to start and close meeting times. Here is what the Project Leader has to do:

-Call members to family meetings

-Set-up the agenda and run the meeting

2) <u>Note Taker</u>: Takes notes at meetings, even the young can do this with a little help from a supporter or a Project Leader!

3) <u>Reminder</u>: This person between sessions helps people remember their goals. Every few sessions they can check in with people and make sure they have completed their weekly goals in a nice way.

4) <u>Cheerer</u>: This is a fun job, you are to give constant Kudos and make sure everyone is feeling ok and supported. They should have a 'kudos' (like a verbal high five) for everyone at family meetings--not just one person. They can also think of rewards that week.

5) <u>Tough Guy/Girl</u>: This is the person who needs to ask the tough questions if you feel someone is not doing their best or needs to work harder. They can also settle compromises during Complaints and Grievances.

Task 2: Figure out who is in what roles first. Fill in the Roles Sheet in the Tools Section.

Task 3: Now that you have assigned your roles, do your family meeting agenda! You can use your family meeting agenda in the Tools Section for help.

FAMILY MEETING NOTES:

Task 4: Next week we will be working on goals. We want you to have a reminder system in place. Brainstorm some ways you can remember goals and homework assignments if you are having trouble remembering.

Reminder System:

-Use a Wall Calendar

-Email Alerts: Set automated email alerts.

-Phone tree: People can call each other to remind.

-Text tree: You text each other reminders.

-Post-it notes

Journal:

Do you think you need a talking stick? Why or why not?

Which role is your favorite, which is your least favorite, why?

Assignments:

__Figure out your reminder system!

__If needed, get a talking stick (literally a stick, a book, a favorite object, etc.)

Session 4: Project the Project

Date:

Today we want you to think about the project as a whole. Now you know a little bit more about how the activities are broken down and you have been practicing family meetings. The discussion questions are also to get each family member to start thinking about goals and self-improvement. For younger family members, this is a good time to explain to them what a goal is and possibly give them examples of previous goals you have had.

Task 1: Do your family meeting agenda, feel free to use your Family Meeting Agenda in the Tools Section for help. Skip Goals section for now.

Family Meeting Notes:

Journal:

1) What do you want to get out of this project?

2) What are you most nervous about?

3) What do you least want to change?

4) Is there a topic you do not want to talk about?

5) Is there something you want to bring up but are nervous to?

Task 2: Go to the Goal Log in the Tools Section and fill in the "Project Goal." What is your family's main goal with this project? Is it just to complete all the lessons? Grow closer? Now that you have a better idea of what the project is about, write down a more specific goal in the Tools Section.

ASSIGNMENTS:

__Next week come prepared to talk about what your life is like in only 5 sentences.

Session 5: Family Snapshot

Date:

A family snapshot is realizing what your family is like right now. This is helpful for two reasons. First, it helps you take a step back and look at what your family looks like right now. This is a great self-assessment. Second, when you look back at your family journal it will be fun to see what your family was like at this moment. You will also end with everyone writing his or her own snapshot.

Task 1: Do your family meeting agenda, feel free to use your Family Meeting Agenda in the Tools Section for help.

Family Meeting Notes:

Task 2: Go to the Family Snapshot sheet in the Tools Section and fill it out for your family.

Journal:

If you have to make a snapshot of the family member to your left, what would you say about them? (Discuss)

ASSIGNMENTS:

__Write down on a blank sheet of paper 3 great perspectives and 3 issues you wish to improve for each area of your life:

*Friends, Family

*Health

*School/Career

*Life

__Reminders and Cheerers should make sure everyone has completed their assignment before the next session.

Session 6: Life Review

Date:

We are getting really close to making goals I promise! The past few sessions have been getting you ready to make some big goal decisions. In this session we are going to help each family member do an overview of the specifics of their lives. Last week you wrote about yourself in only 5 sentences. This week we will look together at the different areas of your life in depth.

Task 1: Do your family meeting agenda, feel free to use your Family Meeting Agenda in the Tools Section for help.

Family Meeting Notes:

Task 2: Discuss the 3 good and 3 bad issues in each are of your life with each other. Help each other make adjustments or think of missing parts.

Journal:

What was harder to talk about the 3 good or the 3 bad?

ASSIGNMENTS:

__On a blank piece of paper please prepare three goals in each of your areas:

*Friends, Family

*Health

*School/Career

*Life

__The Reminder should make sure everyone has done this before the next meeting.

__Figure out your personal planner or calendar. Next week we will be making goals so you will need to have way to remind yourself of your goals and your progress. This can be a phone, a computer calendar, a bulletin board or a wall calendar.

SESSION 7: GOALS

Date:

We are finally here! This is a big day. All of the teens agreed that making goals and having people help you stick to them is one of the most important aspects of being successful. When discussing what makes a good goal, keep in mind that it should be specific enough to reach it, it should be feasible, (or reachable and not too hard to achieve) and quantifiable, meaning you are able to measure whether or not you completed it or not. For example:

"I want to do better in school. "

Is not as good as:

"I want to get B's or higher this semester in school."

Sometimes this session is hard for people. So help each other, be gentle and go slow. If you can only work on one goal at a time this is ok! The cheerers should be supportive and the tough guy/tough girl need to make sure no one is picking goals that are too easy. Also keep in mind everyone works at his or her own pace. What is right for you might not be right for your sibling, parent or child.

Task 1: Do your family meeting agenda, feel free to use your Family Meeting Agenda in the Tools Section for help.

FAMILY MEETING NOTES:

Task 2: Discuss what makes a good goal.

GOAL CRITERIA:

1) Achievable

2) Measurable

3) Specific

4) Breakdown-able

SOME EXAMPLES OF GOOD GOALS:

(You can use these too!)

- Cleaning out the garage

- Fixing the list of "To Fix" items around the house

- Getting above B's this semester

- Getting an A on a term paper/Test/Assignment

- Starting your own blog

- Starting to research college applications

- Getting family finances in order

- Book the summer plans

- Drink at least 8 glasses of water per day

- Make and bring my own lunch to school/work at least 3 times per week

- Have one family dinner per week

- Watch only 1 hour of television per day

- Spend more time with my siblings on weekends

- Do not text during meals

- Organize the office/my desk/my room

- Lose 5 pounds by Christmas

- Call Grandma once per week

Task 3: Discuss three goals in each of your areas:

*Friends, Family

*Health

*School/Career

*Life

We provided an example for you in the tools section. On a blank piece of paper (which you should have gotten for homework last time) have each family member start their own log with each goal and keep it with the workbook and other materials.

The log should look like this for each goal entry:

Goal: **Due Date:**

Action Steps: **Due Dates:**

Task 4: Pick one or two of your goals that you want to work on first. In the Tools Section, write down these goals. You want to pick one goal that is a long-term achievement, like getting higher grades this semester and one that is smaller or in the short term like getting an A on the History term paper. In the tools section, only fill out "Family Member:" and "Goal:" leave "Due Dates" and "Actions Steps" blank for now.

*Tough Guy/Girl needs to challenge goals to make sure that people are not over ambitious or not trying hard enough.

JOURNAL:

Are you excited about achieving your goals, or nervous? Why?

ASSIGNMENTS:

__Begin to think about the steps you need to take to achieve each goal, we call these action steps.

__Write out your goal and put it somewhere where you will see it everyday (bathroom mirrors work great).

Session 8: Action Steps

Date:

Now that you have picked one or two of your goals to work on right now, it is time to break them down and start working! Goals can also be large projects like cleaning out the garage, building the porch, etc. The hardest part about goals is figuring out where to start and how to move onto each step. That is what you will be helping each other with today.

Task 1: Do your family meeting agenda, feel free to use your Family Meeting Agenda in the Tools Section for help.

Family Meeting Notes:

Task 2: Do the action steps for each family member's goals. Help each other figure out what the first steps need to be and the timeline to complete each step.

Journal:

What is important about making goals?

ASSIGNMENTS:

__Put action steps in your personal planner or calendar to complete by due dates.

*<u>Cheerer</u> needs to help people feel great when they finish their first action steps

*<u>Reminder</u> needs to make sure people have begun goals

Session 9: Timelines

Date:

We want you to come up with specific deadlines and timelines for your goals. In this lesson, after you have done your action steps a little you can go back and reevaluate the timeline of where you want your progress to be.

From now on each week you can go through your goals in your family meeting. You will update your goal sheet and check off action steps for each other. We will remind you when it is time to make new goals, but if you complete one of your goals you need to fill it with your next one!

Task 1: Do your family meeting agenda, feel free to use your Family Meeting Agenda in the Tools Section for help.

Task 2: <u>Project Leader:</u> Needs to check off people's goals and action steps in the goal checklist.

Don't forget to keep updating your goal sheet! We also know that you might need more space, you can do this on a blank piece of paper or in a personal journal.

FAMILY MEETING NOTES:

Task 3: Discuss how long it will take to complete each goal and action step.

Task 4: Plot the action steps and goals into a timeline

JOURNAL:

How was doing your first week of action steps, harder or easier than you thought?

Did a family member surprise you with a goal they had or how they completed or did not complete their action step?

ASSIGNMENTS:

__Do your action steps for next week.

Session 10: Do You Know Each Other?

Date:

All of our activities are centered on bonding and getting to know each other. This week is all about getting to know each other on some likes and dislikes. You might be surprised about what you do and do not know about each other...and what you find out!

Task 1: Do your family meeting agenda, feel free to use your Family Meeting Agenda in the Tools Section for help.

Don't forget to keep updating your goal sheet!

Family Meeting Notes:

Task 2: Answer the following questions about each other.

Questions:

1) What is your favorite music band or artist?

2) What is your favorite color?

3) What is the first thing you do in the morning?

4) What is your favorite food?

5) What is something you really want to buy right now?

6) If you could be anything for a job, what would it be?

7) Who is your best friend?

8) What do you love most about yourself?

9) What do you like least about yourself?

10) If you could change one thing about yourself, what would it be?

11) What is your favorite website?

12) Who is your hero?

13) What do you do to relax?

14) What is your pet peeve?

15) Each family member comes up with his or her own question!

JOURNAL:

Who knew you the best, were you surprised?

Who knew you the least?

How did this make you feel?

Who did you know the least?

What can you do to make sure you know this person better?

ASSIGNMENTS:

__Continue Action steps and goals

__Get materials for next week:

*Large thick garbage bags

*Boxes for Charity

*Post-it notes

*Pens

*Paper towels

*Cleaning fluid (Windex)

Session 11: Clean-Out Your Personal Areas

Date:

Part of starting over is cleaning out. We are getting rid of baggage and things that are weighing you down. For this session you are going to clean out your personal areas or bedrooms, in the next few sessions you will work on common areas together.

Task 1: Do your family meeting agenda, feel free to use your Family Meeting Agenda in the Tools Section for help.

Don't forget to keep updating your goal sheet!

Family Meeting Notes:

JOURNAL:

What do you think your biggest challenge will be to clean your personal area?

Task 2: Consider what you want to buy before your clean up to help and to help re-organize once you have cleaned everything out.

<u>To Buy List:</u>

-Trash Cans

-Desk organizers

-Hangers

-Trash Bags

-Drawer organizers

-Hanging shelves for closets

-Shoe racks

-Sticky Tac for pictures

-Bulletin boards for loose papers

-Plastic tubs for supplies and under the bed

-Hooks for the backs of doors and walls for jackets etc.

ASSIGNMENTS:

__Use today or a day before your next session to do the following for your clean up:

*Make Piles: Give-Away, Trash, Re-Organize

*Clean out and throw Away your personal areas (closets, desks, floors, under the bed, etc)

*Reorganize and sort

__Make a trip to charity to donate your charity pile.

SESSION 12: CLEAN OUT COMMON AREAS

Now that your rooms and personal spaces are clean, it is time to clean the common areas. This includes the kitchen, pantries, bathrooms, living room and dining rooms. This should be done together. The reason we had you do your own areas first was to practice for this family bonding experience. They are family areas so the family should clean them up.

Task 1: Do your family meeting agenda, feel free to use your Family Meeting Agenda in the Tools Section for help.

Don't forget to keep updating your goal sheet! Also make sure you are rotating your roles so everyone gets a chance.

FAMILY MEETING NOTES:

Task 3: Think about your launch pads. You want to make sure that each area of your house is designated for a specific purpose. This can really help it stay organized and when you are figuring out where things go.

Answer these Launch Pad Questions and discuss:

1. Where does the mail go?

2. Where do the bills get paid?

3. Where do the groceries go?

4. Where does everyone put his or her dirty clothes?

5. Where does everyone put their backpacks and bags when they walk in the house?

6. Where does everyone get their lunch on the way to school?

7. Where is the toy or game area?

JOURNAL:

Do you think it is fair or unfair to have to clean the family areas?

ASSIGNMENTS:

__Clean the common areas and make piles

__Make a system for how these are going to be maintained with your launch pads.

__Donate giveaways

__Continue on goals!

Session 13: Clean-Out Part II

Date:

We wanted to give you an extra session to clean out and make sure that you are happy with the results of your clean-ups. This is to re-clean or finish cleaning personal and common areas as well as some extra areas.

Task 1: Do your family meeting agenda, feel free to use your Family Meeting Agenda in the Tools Section for help.

Don't forget to keep updating your goal sheet!

Family Meeting Notes:

Task 2: Pick some extra areas to clean out:

__Garage

__Cars

__Attic

__Basement

__Backpacks

__Lockers

JOURNAL:

Did anything about the cleaning out process make you mad?

Did any part of it feel good?

What is the point of cleaning?

ASSIGNMENTS:

__Clean out your extra areas!

Session 14: Re-Stock

Date:

We think it is important for students and parents to have areas that are stocked for homework, projects, bills and mail. If you have this 'launching pad' it helps with organization, less fighting and saves so much time. We want you to take this time to restock your supplies.

Task 1: Do your family meeting agenda, feel free to use your Family Meeting Agenda in the Tools Section for help.

Don't forget to keep updating your goal sheet!

Family Meeting Notes:

Task 2: Look at the Supply Checklist in the Tools Section. Go through this list for each work area you have and make sure each area is stocked.

JOURNAL:

Are you a wandering worker (do you work in many areas around the house)?

Are you a stationary worker (work in one area)?

Are you a hybrid worker (have a main area, but move around sometimes)?

How can you change your study areas to fit the type of worker you are?

ASSIGNMENTS:

__Buy what is missing on your supply list

Session 15: Routine Operating Procedures

Date:

A routine operating procedure is a fancy name for a habit that the family has or does often. The point of making habits into more of a procedure is to get rid of headaches and fighting that happens at a typical time of day or week for your family.

Task 1: Do your family meeting agenda, feel free to use your Family Meeting Agenda in the Tools Section for help.

Don't forget to keep updating your goal sheet!

Family Meeting Notes:

Task 2: Brainstorm times during the week where you often fight, get late or get irritated with other family members. Everyone should have at least one time (these can overlap).

Examples: Morning routines, driving to school, starting homework, after-dinner clean up, etc.

1.

2.

3.

4.

5.

Task 3: Come up with system/tricks for each of your 'trigger times' to become your regular operating procedure. See our examples below:

ROS SCHOOL BACKPACK PACK-UP

If your student is prone to forgetting things at school then it is important for them to have a good routine set-up!

-Check homework lists/or assignment sheets for homework for the night

-Check projects/tests/quizzes in the next few sessions to see if any prep work must be done tonight.

-Go down each subject and check to make sure you have the textbook, notebook, or spiral.

-Do they have their lunchbox/empty water bottle/ sports clothes/ PE clothes/ Instrument/ Laptop etc.

ROS After-School/Homework

-Take a break get a snack (protein and carbs preferably!)

-Big glass of water

-Look in your Planner/Calendar at your HW list and your To Do list and prioritize what you should do first. (I like to either make a list on a separate sheet of paper with checkboxes and the numbered order of when to do what—you can also use a whiteboard).

-Do the hardest things first to get them out of the way while you are still fresh.

-Save the easy homework for later in the evening when you are more tired.

-Remember, that as you finish your homework, hole punch it and file it away, so that you do not leave it at home or misplace it once you get to class.

ROS Mini-Clean-Outs

Schedule in a once a month or if you can, twice per month mini-clean out in their planner. Your kids can do this on their own or with you on Sunday nights. You might want to schedule it into their planner or calendar.

During a mini-clean out they should:

-Clean out all flaps in binders, homework binders, loose papers in textbooks or spirals.

-Clean-Out the backpacks of trash or loose papers

-File Away any papers in the 'to file' session of their files (or create new files if needed).

-Clean off desktop and ins/outboxes.

-Go through Syllabi and Academic Calendar and mark-off any big test, projects or events in the coming months (see test calendars and procrastination tips).

ROS Sunday Nights

At the beginning of the week the student should sit down to look at their schedule for the week. This will help give them an accurate idea of what their time will be like. It is extremely gratifying to start the week knowing that you will have time for everything—including sleep, fun time and homework. Make a to-do list for Sunday nights with them and put it on their desk. It should be a shortened version of this:

1. _____Clean-Out any loose papers, or 'to-file' papers in notebooks or backpack.

2. _____Look through your syllabi at the front part of each classes' divider session and write in important academic dates, for example you would fill-in thing like English Quiz, Math HW due, Physics worksheet due, English Rough Draft in the appropriate sessions. Then highlight with your included highlighter when anything is due or there is an assessment of any kind. This way, you can easily see when there is something important to do so you will not miss studying for a test or turning in an assignment.

3. _____Also look through your class syllabi for the next few weeks and see if there are any projects you need to get started on early. If there is a particularly light session in the week, you can write in that you want to start researching a topic for your science project or history report. This is a great tip for procrastinators!!

4. ___You want to write in any activities and their times so you can see which are your busy sessions. Also check with mom or dad to see if you have any doctor's appointments or family outings that you need to write in. In this way you don't have to find out last minute that you have to go to grandma's birthday party when you need time to study for a test. You can also put any chores your parents want you to do in your "To Do" session of the planner.

5. ___Clean-out your in or outbox on your desk.

ROS: SCHOOL NIGHTS

-File away papers in front and back flaps of homework binder (or just any loose papers)

Give any and all papers to parents

-Go through each homework task in your planner and check off what has been done and make sure each homework is in the correct divider ready to go.

-Pack up backpack (lunch?)

-Look at syllabi and class schedule and make sure all the papers that might be needed for class are in your notebooks.

ROS: Morning Routine

Not everyone needs a morning routine, but if you have a student that is late a lot, or losing papers, you might want to talk to them about the morning routine. Here are a few essentials:

-There should be a prominent clock in every room, they get ready in (especially the bathroom).

-I will sometimes make a laminated checklist of everything they need to do, or bring to the car/bus. See the sample page on the next page!

-Make a bathroom schedule if more than one person shares it—saves a lot of headache, time and fighting.

-Launch pad- all sports gear, water bottles, lunches and backpacks should really be kept in one designated location (preferably near the door).

-One person should be in charge of the ten-minute warning.

Task 4: Think about how you can specifically make the morning easier:

There are various ways to overcome the sleepy feeling that plagues many of us in the morning.

Here are 10 ideas if this is a problem for your student:

* Exercise

* Taking a shower (cold)

* Coffee

* Cooking

* Eating breakfast

* Having an engaging conversation

* Driving (with the windows open)

* Listening to your favorite music

* Reading the newspaper

* Going to sleep early

What are the things you need to do in the morning:

MORNING CHECK LIST:

o_____

o_____

o_____

o_____

o_____

o_____

o_____

o_____

o_____

o_____

o_____

o_____

JOURNAL:

What is your hardest time of the day?

What is your favorite time of the day?

How has implementing and ROS changed this? How could it?

ASSIGNMENTS:

__Implement your ROS for the week. Reminders should help people remember, Cheerers can help complete and project leaders should check off the ROS once completed.

Session 16: Family Goal and Family Challenge

Date:

Now that we are about half way through the program, it is a good time to check in with our goals and think about our big family challenge!

Task 1: Do your family meeting agenda, feel free to use your Family Meeting Agenda in the Tools Section for help.

Don't forget to keep updating your goal sheet!

Family Meeting Notes:

Task 2: Check in with your project goal from the first session. Are you sticking with it? Do you need to make a new one. Decide together whether to continue to complete your family goal or consider making a new one.

Task 3: Plan your Family Challenge! Our teens came up with the idea for a family challenge. A family challenge is an activity that you can do as a family to bond and get a little bit out of your comfort zone. Sit down with your family and think of some things you have always wanted to try or an activity that you think would bring you closer together or to your community. Here are some examples:

- Volunteering at a soup kitchen

- Building a tree house together

- Going on a day walk and camping overnight

- Rock climbing

- Learning to surf

- Taking a cooking class together

JOURNAL:

What do you wish your family was better at?

ASSIGNMENTS:

__Do action steps for family goal

__Begin to plan family challenge

__Continue on personal goals and action steps!

Session 17:
Family Member Alone Time

Date:

In this session we want each family member to book some alone time with each other. This allows you to get close as individuals as well as a family. You might also want to consider having regular mommy-daughter or father-son dates or activities.

Task 1: Do your family meeting agenda; feel free to use your Family Meeting Agenda in the Tools Section for help.

Don't forget to keep updating your goal sheet!

Family Meeting Notes:

JOURNAL:

What are you most looking forward to with each alone date?

What are you least looking forward to?

Task 2: Book alone time with each family member

Task 3: Do a new icebreaker from the icebreaker questions in the Tools Section. Feel free to use these Icebreakers whenever you want to try something new at the beginning of a family meeting.

ASSIGNMENTS:

__Book and do alone time with each family member

Session 18: Mid-Point Check-In

Date:

We are a little more than half way through the sessions and wanted to do a little check-in and review how far we come.

Task 1: Do your family meeting agenda, feel free to use your Family Meeting Agenda in the Tools Section for help.

Family Meeting Notes:

Journal:

Discuss:

One thing you appreciate most about each family member?

One thing you wish they would change?

Something you are afraid of saying?

Task 2: Revisit all goals and action steps. Begin work on a new one.

Task 3: Is everyone OK with roles? Does someone want to swap?

ASSIGNMENTS:

__Family Challenge and Family Alone times should be booked!

SESSION 19: TOUGH LOVE SESSION

Date:

This session might be a little tough, but it will hopefully break down some serious boundaries you are having in your relationships.

Task 1: Do your family meeting agenda, feel free to use your Family Meeting Agenda in the

Tools Section for help.

Don't forget to keep updating your goal sheet!

FAMILY MEETING NOTES:

Task 2: Answer in your personal journal and then discuss answers you are comfortable with talking about:

1) Is there something in your life that you regret?

2) Who is the most successful person you know (are acquainted with)? What qualities make them successful?

3) Who do you think is the most successful historical figure? What qualities make them successful?

4) What would make your child a 'successful' adult?

5) Is your perception of your own child's success the same as it is for other people's children when they are adults?

6) What are the top 3 values you hope your children have?

7) What is one thing you can do this month to consider yourself more successful?

Task 3: Participate in open floor. Open floor is a safe space where anyone in the family can bring up a topic that is concerning them or a person they want to address.

JOURNAL:

Write in your personal journals:

"I feel relieved because…."

"I feel upset because…."

"I feel proud because…"

ASSIGNMENTS:

__Get stationery or paper for next week on gratitude

SESSION 20: GRATITUDE

Date:

It is so important to teach gratitude to kids, remind ourselves to be grateful and help encourage a humble attitude as a family.

Task 1: Do your family meeting agenda, feel free to use your Family Meeting Agenda in the Tools Section for help.

Don't forget to keep updating your goal sheet!

FAMILY MEETING NOTES:

Task 2: Brainstorm and have each family member discuss 3 things that they are grateful for.

Task 3: Each person should list three people they need to thank.

Task 4: Talk about the etiquette of writing a thank you note?

JOURNAL:

Discuss:

Who is one person you should have thanked in your life, but never had the chance to?

ASSIGNMENTS:

__Write thank you notes to your three people.

__Write or type a list of all of the things you are grateful for and put it somewhere you can see it.

__Every time you brush your teeth think of what you have to be excited about (cheerers and reminders can help!)

Session 21: Thanking Each Other

Date:

Last week you worked on being thankful to others, this week we want you to thank the people closest to you—your family!

Task 1: Do your family meeting agenda, feel free to use your Family Meeting Agenda in the Tools Section for help.

Don't forget to keep updating your goal sheet!

Family Meeting Notes:

Journal:

Discuss:

How did the people react who you thanked?

Why is thanking people important?

ASSIGNMENTS:

__Write thank you notes to everyone in your family

Session 22: Dreamlining

Date:

Dreamlining is a way of brainstorming and thinking about what you are passionate about, what you love to do and dreaming big. You are going to help each other think of what you desire most in life and how to achieve it. Dreamlining is really the process of thinking of ideals, goals and desires.

Task 1: Do your family meeting agenda, feel free to use your Family Meeting Agenda in the Tools Section for help.

Don't forget to keep updating your goal sheet!

Family Meeting Notes:

Task 1: Ask each other:

1. What would you do if there were no way you could fail? If you were 10 times smarter than the rest of the world?

2. When you think of the ideal life, what do you think of?

3. What pictures pop into your head when you think about your future self being truly happy?

JOURNAL:

You are going to make a dreamboard. This is a photo collage or a collage of words of all of the things you just brainstormed. You want to sit down and get a big poster board or bulletin board and put pictures, images and words that inspire you to think about your big dreams. Brainstorm what you think you will put on your dreamboard together:

ASSIGNMENTS:

__Get dream board materials

__Finish your dream board

SESSION 23:
FAMILY MEMORY PROJECT

Date:

One of the things that our teens emphasized was the importance of family history and keeping memories together. Today, we are going to talk about your family history.

Task 1: Do your family meeting agenda, feel free to use your Family Meeting Agenda in the Tools Section for help.

Don't forget to keep updating your goal sheet!

FAMILY MEETING NOTES:

Task 2: You are going to do a family memory project. Think of a way you can document your family's history.

Task 3: Discuss: What is your favorite childhood memory

Task 4: Assign parts of your Memory project to each family member, who will write the answers, who will interview extended family members, whether or not you will use videos and who will film them etc.

JOURNAL:

Discuss:

What is one childhood memory you want your children to have?

ASSIGNMENTS:

__Start making your Family Memory Project

__Make sure that for your next session you will be able to turn off all electronics for the day (you might want to peek ahead).

Session 24:
No Electronic Session

Date:

You might have been dreading this day, but having a 24-hour period with no electronics is really important. Being unplugged every once in a while is healthy and good for the family.

Task 1: Do your family meeting agenda, feel free to use your Family Meeting Agenda in the

Tools Section for help.

Don't forget to keep updating your goal sheet!

FAMILY MEETING NOTES:

JOURNAL:

Discuss:

What would your life be like without a cell phone?

What would your life be like without a computer in the house?

Task 2: Do not use electronics today!

Task 3: Try at least 2 other activities that you would never normally do!

Task 4: Book in a no electronic afternoon every few weeks in the family calendar.

ASSIGNMENTS:

__Keep a log of how many hours per week everyone uses the computer. You can put this in a common area and have reminders help keep everyone's hours.

SESSION 25: ONLINE SAFETY

Date:

Online safety is now a part of family life. Not only are family members communicating offline, many communications are now happening online.

Task 1: Do your family meeting agenda, feel free to use your Family Meeting Agenda in the Tools Section for help.

Don't forget to keep updating your goal sheet!

FAMILY MEETING NOTES:

JOURNAL:

Discuss:

How has the Internet changed relationships?

How has the Internet changed privacy?

Task 2: We challenge you to go to Youtube and search "vvanpetten" this is our YouTube channel. We have provided a ton of free videos for you to talk about.

-Watch our videos on why Teens Use Social Networks, Cyberbullying, Cybercitizenship and discuss.

ASSIGNMENTS:

__Make a username and password guide for the family and each person, this is a place where each family member has a list of usernames and passwords so you never lose any.

__Set family parameters about Internet Safety and being online

__Keep a food log for at least two week days and one weekend day (we will talk about this next week)

SESSION 26:
FOOD, HEALTH AND ACTIVITY

Date:

Food and health is also another topic that families often fight about. We wanted to have a place where families could reset and talk about the issues concerning health and nutrition. Use the Food Log Template in the Tools Section.

Task 1: Do your family meeting agenda, feel free to use your Family Meeting Agenda in the Tools Section for help.

Don't forget to keep updating your goal sheet!

FAMILY MEETING NOTES:

Task 2: Discuss your food logs.

Task 3: Project Leader teaches each other the food pyramid. (Use information below and do Internet research on your own if you would like.)

Task 4: Tough Guy/Girl gets to check that everyone gets enough of each food group.

This is an outline of what to eat each session based on the Dietary Guidelines. It's not a rigid prescription, but a general guide that lets you choose a healthful diet that's right for you.

The Pyramid calls for eating a variety of foods to get the nutrients you need and at the same time the right amount of calories to maintain healthy weight.

Use the Pyramid to help you eat better every day...the Dietary Guidelines way. Start with plenty of breads, cereals, rice, pasta, vegetables, and fruits. Add 2-3 servings from the milk group and 2-3 servings from the meat group. Remember to go easy on fats, oils, and sweets, the foods in the small tip of the Pyramid.

WHAT COUNTS AS ONE SERVING?

The amount of food that counts as one serving is listed below. If you eat a larger portion, count it as more than 1 serving. For example, a dinner portion of spaghetti would count as 2 or 3 servings of pasta.

Be sure to eat at least the lowest number of servings from the five major food groups listed below. You need them for the vitamins, minerals, carbohydrates, and protein they provide. Just try to pick the lowest fat choices from the food groups. No specific serving size is given for the fats, oils, and sweets group because you should use them SPARINGLY.

Milk, Yogurt, and Cheese

1 cup of milk or yogurt

1 1/2 ounces of natural cheese

2 ounces of process cheese

Meat, Poultry, Fish, Dry Beans, Eggs, and Nuts

2-3 ounces of cooked lean meat, poultry, or fish

1/2 cup of cooked dry beans,

1 egg, or 2 tablespoons of peanut butter count as 1 ounce of lean meat

Vegetable

1 cup of raw leafy vegetables

1/2 cup of other vegetables, cooked or chopped raw

3/4 cup of vegetable juice

Fruit

1 medium apple, banana, orange

1/2 cup of chopped, cooked, or canned fruit

3/4 cup of fruit juice

Bread, Cereal, Rice, and Pasta

1 slice of bread

1 ounce of ready-to-eat cereal

1/2 cup of cooked cereal, rice, or pasta

JOURNAL:

Discuss:

Was the food and health week easier or harder than other weeks, why?

Do you have any new health goals after discussing food with the family?

ASSIGNMENTS:

__Clean out your pantry together

__Go grocery shopping together and see if you can come up with some healthy snacks.

__Keep a food log again and see if your food groups are better

Session 27: Teach Each Other

Date:

One of the best ways to feel confident is to teach others about something or how to do something you are really good at. In this lesson each family member will prepare a lesson on something they are good at and want to teach the other family members.

Task 1: Do your family meeting agenda, feel free to use your Family Meeting Agenda in the Tools Section for help.

Don't forget to keep updating your goal sheet!

Family Meeting Notes:

Task 1: Discuss:

"What is something you are really good at?"

"What is something you wish you could learn?"

"What is a skill you really admire in each family member?"

Task 2: Each family member should pick one skill they can teach the rest of the family that everyone would have an interest in learning.

Examples:

-Cooking

-A sport

-Knitting

-Painting

-How to give a presentation

-Fixing cars

-How to use crayons

JOURNAL:

Discuss:

Why do you think it is important to teach?

What is something you have loved teaching in the past? If you have nothing, what did you not enjoy?

ASSIGNMENTS:

__Prepare, research and get materials for your lesson

Session 28: Teach!

Date:

Today, or during this session you will teach each other the lesson you have prepared.

Task 1: Do your family meeting agenda, feel free to use your Family Meeting Agenda in the Tools Section for help.

Don't forget to keep updating your goal sheet!

Family Meeting Notes:

Task 2: Teach each other your lessons.

JOURNAL:

Discuss:

How did it feel to be taught by other (possibly younger) members of your family?

How did it feel to teach?

ASSIGNMENTS:

__Update goals and roles again

Session 29: Future Selves

Date:

We are getting close to the end of our sessions and our teens wanted to put together a lesson specifically on deciding the future.

Task 1: Do your family meeting agenda, feel free to use your Family Meeting Agenda in the Tools Section for help.

Don't forget to keep updating your goal sheet!

Family Meeting Notes:

Task 1: Discuss:

"Where do you see yourself in 5 years? What is different? What is the same?"

"Where do you see yourself in 20 years? What is different? What is the same?"

Task 2: Write letters to yourself in 20 years, what advice would you give yourself?

JOURNAL:

Discuss:

Are you scared or excited for the future?

Do you like or dislike change?

Why would or wouldn't you ask for help from a family member if you were struggling with something?

ASSIGNMENTS:

__Write short letters to each of your family members in 20 years. What would you say to them?

__Gather at least 2 materials per person to put in a time capsule.

SESSION 30: TIME CAPSULE

Date:

This is our last session together. We want you to make a time capsule! This will be great to open up 5, 10 or 15 years down the line and a great way to keep memories.

Task 1: Do your family meeting agenda, feel free to use your Family Meeting Agenda in the Tools Section for help.

Don't forget to keep updating your goal sheet!

FAMILY MEETING NOTES:

Task 2: Go get the item that is most important to the family member on your right and discuss the choices.

Task 3: Present 2 items each person would like to put in their time capsule and why

Task 4: Build your time capsule (include the letters). Consider putting in this book or your journal entries.

JOURNAL:

Discuss:

How does it feel to be done with the sessions? Sad? Relieved?

What do you plan on taking away with you from this process?

Conclusion

We are done!

Now it is time to put all of these into practice.

- Hold regular family meetings

We hope there are many different things that you have taken away from this process. One of them might be to continue having family meetings. There are tons of Icebreakers in the Tools Section and to keep checking in with each other is essential to the bonding process.

- Make family goals

During your family meetings we really encourage you to make family goals. This gives you something to work towards and achieving and celebrating the success of the family goal is the best part!

- Make personal goals

We also strongly encourage you to make personal goals and to help each other do this. The whole point of making roles—the project leader, the cheerer, the tough guy and the reminder—is because we all play these roles at different times in our families. When you keep supporting each other to make goals you can bring back the roles that are needed to best encourage the other person.

- Love

We hope that working through these lessons has helped you get to know each other, reconnect and most of all, feel the love you have for one another. Even in moments of fighting, disagreements and upset, the love will always be there.

To your success,

Vanessa Van Petten and the Radical Teen Team

For more free resources updated sessions, icebreakers and free videos check out RadicalParenting.com. The learning does not have to stop here!

TOOLS SECTION FAMILY JOURNAL

Here are all of the tools and resources to go along with your activities. Please use them as you move through the sessions.

Our Family Meeting Agenda:

1)

2)

3)

4)

5)

6)

GOAL LOG

Project Goal:

(Do for each family member)

Example:

Family Member: *Marci*

Goal 1: *Get higher than B's this semester.*   **Due Date:** *Report Card 12/09*

Action Steps: **Due Dates:**

___*Find a peer tutor at school for math*   07/09/09*

___*Meet with all of my teachers during office hours once per*

month (Get office hour schedules and meet with them this week) 12/09/09

___*Finish homework before I go online   Ongoing, mom checks each night*

*Each family member should keep their own log on a blank piece of paper and keep it with the notebook the Project Leader can check off everyone's actions steps and goals each week.

Fill out the top of each person's log like this:

Family Member:

Goal 1:   **Due Date:**

Action Steps: **Due Dates:**

Goal 2:   **Due Date:**

Action Steps: **Due Dates:**

Roles Sheet

Fill in the names of family members below.

<u>Project Leader</u>:

    Sessions 3-6:

    Sessions 7-10:

    Sessions 10-13:

    Sessions 14-17:

    Permanent Role (leave blank until decided):

<u>Note Taker</u>:

    Sessions 3-6:

    Sessions 7-10:

    Sessions 10-13:

    Sessions 14-17:

    Permanent Role (leave blank until decided):

<u>Reminder</u>:

Sessions 3-6:

Sessions 7-10:

Sessions 10-13:

Sessions 14-17:

Permanent Role (leave blank until decided):

<u>Cheerer</u>:

Sessions 3-6:

Sessions 7-10:

Sessions 10-13:

Sessions 14-17:

Permanent Role (leave blank until decided):

<u>Tough Guy/Girl</u>:

Sessions 3-6:

Sessions 7-10:

Sessions 10-13:

Sessions 14-17:

Permanent Role (leave blank until decided):

CONTRACT:

Date:

I am willing to work with my family together with the following agreed upon guidelines:

* I am willing to be open-minded to trying new things, activities and ideas.

* I will be open-minded to my family member's feelings, criticisms and advice to the best of my ability.

* I want to try to break habits and cycles that do not benefit myself or other family members.

* I promise to be honest with others about my feelings and boundaries.

* I want to make a fresh start.

*I will, to the best of my ability do all of the assignments for each segment.

*I will try to keep a journal and answer the prompts at least once per each segment.

*I will ask for help if I need it.

*I will participate in the family meetings and check-ins.

*

*

*

Signed by each family member:

FAMILY SNAPSHOT

Please fill in the following together.

Date:

Where do you live:

Describe your house:

What is your family like?

Do you have any pets? Describe them:

What is your typical family schedule on a weekday?

What do you do on the weekends?

Do a family snapshot for each person:

Write no more than 5 sentences about who you are. Make sure to include your name, your age, where you go to school or work, what your favorite and least favorite things are and any other interesting facts about you.

Supply Checklist:

-Trash Cans

-Desk organizers

-Hangers

-Trash Bags

-Drawer organizers

-Hanging shelves for closets

-Shoe racks

-Sticky Tack for pictures

-Bulletin boards for loose papers

-Plastic tubs for supplies and under the bed

-Hooks for the backs of doors and walls for jackets etc.

-Plenty of plugs (extension cords?)

-Pens

-Pencils

-Eraser

-Pencil Sharpener (if they have those kinds of pencils)

-Lead (if they have those kinds of pencils)

-Correction fluid or tape

-Crayons/Markers/Colored Pencils (one basic set for school projects that will not be used for crafts)

-Stapler and Staples

-Tape

-Glue

-Scissors

-Hole Puncher (a bigger one that can do more than 3 sheets at a time)

-Paper clips

-Ruler

-Rubber Bands

-Index Cards (in three or four colors)

-Calculator

-Highlighters

-Post-it Notes

-Tabs

-Reinforcements

-White Paper

-Lined Paper

-Glue

-Pencil case for school (get a soft one, not a hard case)

-Book stand* (can get this anywhere and it will save their necks)

-Inbox/Outbox* (This will not work on every desk, but find it is a helpful place to put all 'need to deal with' papers, and you can go through it with them every time you see them)

-Backpack

-printer

-ink

-Blank CDs

-External Hardrive

(If you want it)

-Protractor

-Compass

-Book Covers

-Calendar

-Bulletin Board and Pushpins

-Drawer organizer

-lined pads

-dictionary

-thesaurus

-report covers

-Poster Board (If they have a place to keep it, I find there are always last minute projects that need poster board)

-Desk calendar (talk to them about desk calendar vs. computer calendar vs. planner—later this lesson).

-Doodle Notebook

-graph paper

<u>Depends on School Schedule and Requirements</u>: (see "School Central" Lesson)

-Extra Binders

-Extra Spirals

-More Dividers

-Paper folders

-Poly Pocket Folders

-Sheet protectors

ICEBREAKERS

1. Personality Tests

Teens love to get to know themselves and their friends with fun personality tests like this color quiz.

2. Human Bingo

Make a bunch of paper squares or flashcards with a name of a person playing and a question. The players must find that teen and ask him or her to sign the square and answer the question. The first person to get 5 squares done wins a candy bar.

3. Interviews

Each teen interviews the teen next to him or her for 2 minutes and then introduces the teen to the group. I would give out a list of questions for them to work off of.

4. Would you rather...?

Gross and funny questions of would you rather are great party starters. Have one side of the room be one answer and the other side be the other answer and have them switch sides depending on their choice and then they can easily see who would rather eat their own puke or eat a dead bug.

5. I never ever

Give each of teen in a circle 10 jellybeans or pennies. In turn, each teen tells something they have never done. Anyone who has done it gives the speaker one of his or her pennies. After going around the circle twice, the person with the most jellybeans or pennies wins. For example: I have never traveled outside to Europe. I have never eaten Thai food. I have never played the piano.

6. Two Truths and a Lie

In turn, teens each tell two true things and one false thing about themselves. The group tries to guess which one is the lie.

7. Famous People

Tape names of famous people on the teens' backs. They have to ask each other yes or no questions until they can guess who they are. For example: Am I a man? Am I a singer? The trick is the can only ask one question to each person.

8. Human Pizza

This works well for a larger group of teens. Make cards for all the ingredients of a pizza, as many copies as needed so each teen is an ingredient. Tape the cards to the teens' backs and they must assemble themselves in small groups, each with all the ingredients and toppings of a pizza by asking each other yes and no questions.

9. Memory Tray

Put out objects on a tray and people have to list all that was on theirs after only looking for 30 seconds, bonus points for descriptions.

10. Password Game

How well do you know each other's minds? Think of one word and then say another one word clue. For example, if you wanted them to guess 'rose' you could say flower and hope the first flower they think of is a rose.

11. Knots

Have everyone clump together and hold hands, then make them work out a circle without breaking hands.

12. Shoes in a Pile

Have everyone put their shoes in a pile, people get to pick one and then find the match.

13. Toilet Paper

Pass around a toilet paper roll, have teens take as little or as much as they want then they have to tell something about themselves for every piece of toilet paper they have.

14. Lines

Have them line up by birthday order, age, and height without talking!

15. Secret Lingo

No one can speak or hold up numbers with their hands, but everyone is given a number and they have to put themselves in correct order using a secret language they make-up.

Icebreaker Questions:

1. If you had to give every human being one quality, what would it be and why?

2. Do you have any recurring dreams? Describe them?

3. What is the meanest thing someone could say to you?

4. If you could be a famous athlete, actor, writer or musician which would you choose and why? (It is fun to guess what the other people in the group will say before divulging answers)!

5. If you were invisible where would you go and what would you do?

6. If your life was made into a movie, who would play you? why?

7. If you could invent one thing what would it be?

8. What is the greatest song ever written?

9. Do you believe in heaven? What does yours look like? Is it different for everyone?

10. What is the most important quality for a boss to have?

11. If you could know one thing about the future, what would it be?

12. DARE: Eat your favorite food, before you swallow spit it out and re-eat it (teens love playing the truth or Dare Kubit2Me and I don't think I laughed so hard in a long time, this was my favorite one–and the grossest)

13. How do you choose your friends?

14. What is the first thing you notice about a person?

15. What do you think is the biggest problem in the United States and Why?

16. Describe the most beautiful thing you have ever seen.

17. What would the cover of your autobiography look like if it could not be a picture of you or your family?

18. If you could trade places with anyone in the world who would it be and why? How about someone in your family?

19. Do you ever talk to yourself? When and what do you say?

20. Tell the group (or other person) the most attractive thing about the person on your right.

ICEBREAKERS TO GET TO KNOW EACH OTHER'S PERSONALITIES:

How did dad propose?

What has been the best day of your life so far?

What has been the worst day?

What is the biggest goal you have ever achieved?

When were you really afraid of something?

What are you most proud of?

Food Log

Name: _____   Day_____

Time: **Food:**

Day_____

Time: **Food:**

ABOUT THE AUTHOR

Vanessa, age 24, from Los Angeles, CA loves helping parents and youth and wrote her first nationally acclaimed parenting book from the kid's perspective at the age of 16.

This book was also written with 20 of the Radical Parenting teen writers, meet a few of them:

Sarah, age 16 from Kansas City, Kansas who loves writing, her friends and the swim team.

Brad, age 14 from Sacramento, California who loves to skateboard, listen to music and hang out online.

Chelsea, age 17 from Cambridge, England who is obsessed with poetry and her dog, snuffles.

Marni, age 12 from Denver, Colorado loves Club Penguin, can't wait to be on Facebook and wishes her mom let her get an iPod.

Mark, age 17 from Washington, D.C. is applying to College, loves building cars with his dad and wants to be a race car driver.

Vanessa Van Petten works with thousands of teens everyday. She is one of the nation's youngest experts, or 'youthologists' on parenting and adolescents. She wrote her first parenting book from the teen's perspective, called "You're Grounded!," when she was just 17. After winning the Mom's Choice Award in 2009 and launching her popular parenting blog, she is now on a national speaking tour, reaching out to both parents and teenagers talking about what young people really wish adults knew about them.

Her blog: RadicalParenting.com, which she writes with 75 other teenage writers from ages 12 to 20, is read by thousands of teens and adults daily and has been featured on hundreds of other parenting sites around the web as the only teen written parenting blog. She has been featured on CNN, CBS Miami and Fox New York and has been in the Wall Street Journal, Teen Vogue, Atlanta Insite Magazine and the World Journal. She has been an expert on numerous radio programs including Playboy Radio, KBUR, WCOJ Philadelphia and more for giving a young perspective on awesome parenting. She is now 24 and living in Los Angeles, CA.